P.S.
PRAY the same for Me

Release, Grow, and Inspire

MARQUITA SMITH

BALBOA.
PRESS

A DIVISION OF HAY HOUSE

Balboa Press books may be ordered through booksellers or by contacting:

Balboa Press
A Division of Hay House
1663 Liberty Drive
Bloomington, IN 47403
www.balboapress.com
1-(877) 407-4847

Because of the dynamic nature of the Internet, any web addresses or
links contained in this book may have changed since publication and
may no longer be valid. The views expressed in this work are solely those
of the author and do not necessarily reflect the views of the publisher,
and the publisher hereby disclaims any responsibility for them.

The author of this book does not dispense medical advice or prescribe the use
of any technique as a form of treatment for physical, emotional, or medical
problems without the advice of a physician, either directly or indirectly. The
intent of the author is only to offer information of a general nature to help you
in your quest for emotional and spiritual well-being. In the event you use any
of the information in this book for yourself, which is your constitutional right,
the author and the publisher assume no responsibility for your actions.

Any people depicted in stock imagery provided by Thinkstock are models,
and such images are being used for illustrative purposes only.
Certain stock imagery © Thinkstock.

ISBN: 978-1-4525-7694-7 (sc)
ISBN: 978-1-4525-7696-1 (hc)
ISBN: 978-1-4525-7695-4 (e)

Library of Congress Control Number: 2013911687

Printed in the United States of America.

Balboa Press rev. date: 07/01/2013

For Janet Matthews Moore, Beatrice Hardwick, Snowdie Flowers, and Lillian Ann Martinson, whose hips carried me, whose shoulders held me up, and whose prayers I've been the beneficiary of. May this book serve as a release to you and provide you rest. Thank you for releasing me.

The songs of all my great-grandmothers and the dreams of all my great-grandfathers, the dance of Heaven and Earth all live in me, all live in me!

—Ricki Byars Beckwith

CONTENTS

PREFACE

Some things are so deeply rooted that if not removed from their origin will continue to grow in different seasons.

—Marquita Smith

Once you open yourself up to the journey, all the guidance and resources you need magically appear, so I wasn't surprised when I met with my mentor and spiritual confidant, Dr. Guldal Caba, PhD, and she asked me to go home and pray for the four to six generations of women in my family who came before me and, in my prayer, ask that they do the same for me. She told me that a lot of the things I had been dealing with was just unfinished business that they had not dealt with—had not handled. I didn't know what I was going to say or how I was going to communicate with these *generations*, but I agreed. When I got home, I jumped in the shower, and I remembered what she had asked me to do. So I began to pray, and it went something like this: "I pray that you have prosperity; pray the same for me. I pray that you dismiss your fears and are able to achieve all that you have ever imagined; please pray the same for me." After a few seconds something took over, and these deeply rooted, soul-aching prayers flooded my heart and my mind and fell off of my tongue; they went rushing to the door of my consciousness for their overdue release.

I felt a tremendous release, as if my soul had exhaled. After that experience, I could hear differently, think differently. It was as if someone had hit the reset button.

The next morning at around 5:30 a.m., I sat at my computer and began to write these prayers. What came up for me was that there may be others who need to be released or who need some sort of ritual that they can do to free themselves from old programming, old thought patterns—people who need to connect themselves to the past in order to disconnect themselves and live in the present.

We are inherently linked to our past. I understood this in theory and in a spiritual sense. This isn't a new concept. It has been discussed, written about, and theorized for ages in different religions and spiritual practices; however, I dismissed its relevance in my life. I dismissed the connection between how I thought about, felt, dealt with, and processed things emotionally and how the generations of women in my family did the same.

I eerily began to see similarities in my strengths as well as my constricting weaknesses.

This book is dedicated to women of all races, ethnicities, and socioeconomic statuses who are willing to reach back and bless prior generations in order to release and free themselves.

It's taken me two years of courageous self-reflection to start the journey and have the courage to write this book. I am well certified in the work of my soul, my journey, and my enlightenment. I am just a woman who wants to bless the generations of women who came before me, to nurture and pray for them—to give them what it is that they didn't get while here in the physical, to release them and me so that I may finish the business that was left unfinished.

LETTER FROM MY MOM

It was July 4, 2002, a week to the day before my twenty-sixth birthday. I had fallen asleep on the couch and woken up from an all-too-real dream.

My mother, my sister, and I were fleeing from a burning house. We were scurrying like mice women, trying to gather our belongings, when all of a sudden my mother looked at me and said, "You aren't coming with me." "What are you saying to me, Ma?" "You can't come!" As if she were making her great escape from years of bondage, she ran out of the door and jumped from the porch into the arms of women fully clad in all white. They lifted her up to the heavens, and then I awoke. Startled, I called her hospital room, where she had been lying since her body had betrayed her again, this time with a vengeance. It had spread from her breast to her spleen, to her spine, and then to her stomach. I got no response. Frantic, I called again. My act of persistence reminded me of how I would call her office as a child to ask her ordinary questions like, "Can I make a grilled cheese sandwich?" "I finished my homework; can I watch TV now?" "When are you coming home?"

1

Except now, it wasn't as mundane as that. Now, if she didn't pick up, I knew she would never, ever pick up.

The kind of never that's eternal and the kind of eternal that is everlasting—those are the kinds I wasn't ready for. Finally, after an hour or so, she answered.

I told her about my dream. She laughed and said, "You know we have always been connected in that way. Just keep paying attention." "Okay, I will." "It's okay, and you know I'm not afraid to die, right?" *But I'm afraid for you to die*, I thought. "Be strong, please. If you aren't all right, I won't be all right she said." I said okay, cringing at my unauthentic self. There was a moment of silence, and then it just came up and out like a volcano erupting, hurried and hot. "Can you at least write me a letter or something?" The momentary silence was extremely loud. I could hear she was out of breath; she said she needed a nap. "Go on your birthday trip now, and I'll see you when you get back." *Write me a letter*, proclaimed and solidified, in my mind, that she was going to write me one.

I went with my husband and our best friends to the most breathtaking place I have ever visited in my life—Portofino, an Italian fishing village that's famous for its harbor. We lived on a boat and slept at sea. I kept thinking about her and what words I would say the next time we spoke, what I would tell her about my trip.

But that week I was away, she went away.

My sister called my husband the day before my birthday and told him she had passed. My husband told me the day after my birthday. I guess he didn't want me to grieve that day; I guess he wanted me to have my mother on my birthday because he knew I would grieve every single day the rest of my life.

We flew back to Alabama and buried her and then began the dreaded task of packing up her things.

As I was clearing out her chestadrawer (chest of drawers), I remembered the letter. It was a whirlwind after that. I combed every inch of her room. I searched every old purse, shoe box, and file cabinet and spent nights going through all of her piles and piles of books to see where she could have possibly left my letter. Nothing was left unturned. I knew that she had remembered, and my letter was somewhere in this house. I discovered a junk drawer containing tons of receipts, bills, and divorce decrees—I hadn't known my parents were divorced twice.

There were old licenses and titles to cars, but no title that said, "To My Daughter."

I kept at it.

I mined and excavated for hours that turned into days, as if my life depended on it; it did—as if the letter held for me momentous insight into a last good-bye, a last *I love you*, how to take care of my self, lessons I shouldn't forget, how to be a mother, my eternal letter to keep now that she wasn't here. After all, I was a twenty-six-year-old motherless child who needed to be walked through life. I found nothing. I found emptiness.

With her pots and pans, her books, her tattered Bible, and the junk drawer in tow, I headed back to New York.

Two weeks later my father died. She wouldn't have liked that. But he was too brokenhearted to live without her. We knew that.

I knew it was coming. I wished he'd stayed a little longer, but I guess the only thing worse than losing my mother was losing the love of his life; I still had mine.

After cleaning out my father's house back in Alabama and revisiting my mother's storage, it wasn't there either. I decided it was time to give up my quest for the letter.

Years later, my husband and I had a baby boy. We were getting settled into our new home, and I began to unpack my mother's stuff: the books, the pots and pans, and the junk drawer. I found poetry scribbled on driving directions to Florida; quotes, sayings, and prayers on the corners of recipes for the best sour cream pound cake and southern fudge; and index cards with Bible verses written on them. I read all of the leaflets she kept, the get-well-soon cards, and each precious note to self she had written. The sight of her handwriting was a catharsis for my aching soul.

And then I came upon all the letters I had ever written to her. They were letters that I would sneak under her bedroom door or drop in her purse. Frivolous, adolescent, and teenaged pleas of permission and forgiveness littered the bottom of the junk drawer that I had been carrying with me all these years—my letters.

Then it dawned on me that the letter I had been searching for was right in front of me; I was her letter that she had left behind, but not delivered how I imagined it to be.

But I finally got it. I was, I am, her letter.

I am the physical imprint of her journey. It became time for me to stop searching and start my own journey, using the things she left behind as a road map to releasing, growing and inspiring.

I Come to Me

Before I arrived, there were things I wanted for me,

things that did not yield simplicity.

For all of the things in this world that I own,

none do I cherish so much that I cannot leave them alone.

The peace and joy that I found within me

was always there; I failed to see.

The hunger and thirst to be secure

were stored in my pantry of insecurity.

As I opened the door and brushed doubt aside,

from the sleep of systematic ruins I began to arise,

lifting the veil laid by offensive intruders

that sometimes causes the mind to inhabit worldly polluters, fighting the battle to win the war in the spirit,

increased power coming forth as He allowed it.

I emerged from the cocoon that sheltered

destruction in my path . . . into a realm pleasing

to Him that would give the peace that lasts.

This is the place where I needed to be,

one that enabled me to finally see

that at long last being found, I come to me.

—Janet Matthews Moore

I pray that you always seek to understand yourself and, no matter how painful self-reflection is, you always partake in it.

I pray that you are free to create and be the most magnificent version of yourself. Be free to have goals and continue to stretch until they are accomplished or until your inner voice tells you it is time to release and start fresh.

I pray that you are devoted to your goals and, even when self-doubt creeps in, you are able to push through. Know that discouragement and doubt will surface, but wade through.

I pray that you have patience.

I pray that you know that whatever you set your mind and heart to will come to you. Stay the course and be as diligent as a bird feeding its young.

I pray that your heart and mind remain open so that you are able to see your dreams realized, even if they don't show up wrapped in the package you intended.

I pray that you are comfortable in your own skin and that you are confident enough to allow others to be comfortable in theirs.

I pray you cry when you want to cry, laugh when you want to laugh, get mad when you want to, and be silent when you need to.

I pray that you are gentle with yourself. Nurture you.

I pray that you trust yourself. Give yourself permission to be right and allow yourself to be wrong.

I pray that you know that being wrong doesn't mean you aren't smart.

I pray that when you make mistakes you learn from them. Don't beat yourself up relentlessly.

I pray that you can admit when you are wrong.

I pray that you embrace your weaknesses in the same measure as you do your strengths. Find the blessing and gifts in your frailties and insecurities.

I pray that you can look yourself in the mirror and love what you see.

I pray that when you need help you are courageous enough to ask for it.

I pray that you don't worry whether you say or do the right things and just live from the heart, never second-guessing your every thought or feeling.

I pray that you forgive yourself, however many times it takes.

I pray that you know your worth and that you don't have to look outside of yourself for acceptance.

I pray that you do not place yourself on the "sale rack." Value who you are and have enough benevolence for self that you come to your own defense.

I pray that you are self-reliant and that you trust your instincts.

I pray that you are anchored in security, self-acceptance, and belief in yourself.

I pray that you don't put yourself on anyone else's timeline.

I pray that you are able to believe in you and not in who others believe you to be. Remember that they are limited in their knowledge of your inner workings.

I pray that you aren't afraid to lose. Take risks and learn from your losses.

I pray that you practice fidelity with yourself. Know that in order to expect and accept faithfulness from others, you have to be faithful to you.

I pray that you understand that everything that has happened and will happen to you is by design. These experiences are moving you into who you are to become in this world. Don't resist, breathe deep, and expect and accept growth.

I pray that you remain present and mindful every day.

I pray that you recognize your blessings and that your heart isn't so heavy that you are blinded by the weight of it and can't see what's in front of you.

I pray that you can have joy through your sorrow.

I pray that you know when it's time to let go. Whether it's a person, a job, or a way of thinking, know when enough is enough.

I pray that you know that everyone in your life mirrors aspects of who you are. They are your greatest treasures because they show you everything you need to work on or acknowledge yourself for.

I pray that you are open enough to see the good and the bad in this reflection and that you are accepting of these different facets of self.

I pray that you don't crumble under pressure; just lean into it, and know that there is a lesson.

I pray that you recognize when you are in your *story* and that you are able to decipher what's fact and what's not. Be courageous enough to change it, if it no longer serves you. Be committed to pulling yourself out of your story.

I pray that you recognize when you are projecting. Own, embody, and find the endowment in your projections. If done, emotional riches will be sure to flow!

I pray that you aren't easily shaken by disturbances—internal or external.

I pray that you can peer through the glass of anger, embrace it, and use it as a lens to guide you to peace.

I pray that when things get rough, you fight. Go to war to keep your sacred landscape self-protected.

I pray that you don't respond to evil with evil.

I pray that you allow yourself to explore and learn new things. I pray that your curiosity lives and breathes for as long as you are on this earth.

I pray that you pay attention to what is going on around you and use your experiences and the world as your classroom, not shying away from any course.

I pray that you are open to the unexpected and embrace the possibility that there is a lesson in everything.

I pray that you don't beat yourself up for the decisions you make to better yourself.

I pray that you stand true to the convictions of your heart. Don't shy away from your spirituality for fear of ridicule.

I pray that you let go of the need for acceptance. Make sure you are giving yourself the acceptance you crave from others.

I pray that you acknowledge how great you are.

I pray that you are drowning in confidence.

I pray that you recognize how beautiful you are.

I pray that you can see yourself, in all of your glory, as a wonderful creation of the universe.

I pray that you graciously accept compliments and that you don't steal this reward from your spirit with reasons why you don't deserve them.

I pray that if you feel you have something to say in this world, you say it and refuse to be silenced.

I pray that you have integrity when others are watching and, most importantly, when they are not.

I pray that you are immunized against fear.

I pray that you learn how to get out of your own way.

I pray that you are comfortable while on your own path and know that this is your journey you are authoring. Don't give the pen to someone else.

I pray that you have undisturbed peace.

I pray that you strive for emotional maturity so that when situations become difficult, you stay true to your core and shift negative emotions so that they don't get the best of you. Learn from them, but don't be taken down by them.

I pray that you free yourself from incessant worry and negativity.

I pray that you know that everything you need, all the answers and directions, are within. Trust yourself enough to listen to the advice of your soul.

I pray that you are comfortable with expressing your needs and wants.

I pray that you know that there is power in silence. You don't have to be audible to be heard.

I pray that you have a mind of your own.

I pray that you are okay with being misunderstood. Everyone won't always be mentally, emotionally, or spiritually where you are, and they may never be. Be okay with this.

I pray that you are able to recognize when habits, or ways of thinking or being, no longer work for you.

I pray that you have the courage to question, always.

I pray that you understand that you don't have to be accepted by the majority. Embrace your individuality.

I pray that you nourish yourself daily, especially in your moments of discontent.

I pray that you are able to accept and honor your past.

I pray that shame doesn't occupy any room in your house of life.

I pray that you realize that when you neglect yourself, neglect will trickle down to other aspects and people in your life.

I pray that you know the importance of being authentically you. Authentic love is deeply rooted and tied to the authenticity of the love you have for yourself.

Please pray the same for me.

YOUR PRAYERS

YOUR PRAYERS

YOUR PRAYERS

YOUR PRAYERS

YOUR PRAYERS

YOUR PRAYERS

YOUR PRAYERS

_____

_____

_____

_____

_____

_____

_____

_____

_____

_____

_____

_____

_____

_____

_____

_____

_____

_____

YOUR PRAYERS

YOUR PRAYERS

YOUR PRAYERS

YOUR PRAYERS

YOUR PRAYERS

WHEN WISDOM SPEAKS

Yielding to the voice of the soul,

coming forward with a force so bold,

hearing that which has been spoken and again retold . . .

Do not be found remaining foolish,

laughing at wisdom after receiving worldly schooling.

Receive divine knowledge, which causes

one to see wrong in self.

Be dependable and obliging and on others do not welch.

Men have changed the name of sin

to compromise errors that lurk within,

whereby blocking enlightenment,

blinded by the one from darkness sent.

The fool hates wisdom that gives self-control,

which is more precious than silver and gold.

Each being is responsible for setting his mind on understanding,

yet false revelations to him are more demanding.

The materialistic mind is born of the flesh.

Hold on to vain beliefs rather than relinquish.

Gluttony for the perishable . . .

receiving the light becomes impossible.

Aim to be worthy of being approved;

let not darkness and ignorance rule.

For in this great land called earth,

one must compel self to hunger and thirst

for the wisdom that fills an empty heart

and causes evil transgressions to depart.

To all He gives free will to choose,

in that receiving truth, to be freed and not lose.

Give not way to self-aggrandizement

and accumulations of unneeded wealth.

For these are the spoils of mankind . . .

shortcomings that breed lovers of self.

Let your spirit soar and your mind reach

for divine knowledge given when wisdom speaks.

—Janet Matthews Moore

I pray when wisdom melodically sings to your soul, you listen intently to every verse.

I pray that you are aware and open to the idea that wisdom can come in many different forms, different ages, ethnicities, and religions; keep your eyes peeled and ears open.

I pray that you exercise and stretch your spiritual muscle daily, not just when you are experiencing a cramp in your life.

I pray that you clean up in the present what needs to be cleaned up from the past.

I pray that you are strong enough to endure during times of perceived lack.

I pray that prosperity refuses to hide from you and that it reveals itself to you in all its glorious forms.

I pray that you are committed to and keep your focus on prosperity and abundance, not lack and scarcity.

I pray that you understand there is enough to go around. No one has what is designed for you. Be happy for others when good befalls them. We all are one.

I pray that you don't let your financial situation dictate and undermine your core.

I pray that you view life's issues with your heart and mind's eye, only examining them just enough to feel and learn; release quickly.

I pray that you are bold enough to relax, release, and inspire.

I pray that you learn to forgive, no matter the offense.

I pray that you fight your own battles. Be guided by your own cause.

I pray that you don't define yourself by your circumstances or your experiences.

I pray that you live a life with no regrets and know that where you are is exactly where you are to be. You are divinely mentored.

I pray that you know that no matter what, you are loved and that you belong. There is a "memory foam" spot in the universe that only fits the slant and the curve of your soul.

I pray that you focus on what is right in your life and not what is wrong, even if that list is short. Know that focusing on the positive will bring you more of the same. Keep adding to your list.

I pray that when you feel the rope of bitterness tugging at you, you let go.

I pray you let go of the need for others to understand.

I pray that you understand the power of your thoughts and your speech. Think right and speak right.

I pray that you understand that people pleasing robs you of your power. Look to please and be pleasing in the eyes of the Divine (God), which in turn will allow you to be pleasing to yourself.

I pray that you strive not only to wear the crown but also to embody what the crown represents. Yearn to operate at your highest frequency possible.

I pray that while on your journey of enlightenment you do not force others off of the road with your flashing high beams of consciousness. Everyone will not drive like you drive, go in the same direction as you, or move at the same speed. The goal for us all is to learn how to drive in a way that keeps everyone who is on the road, on the road. Remember you were once a beginner driver also.

I pray that when you are on your "soul work" journey you understand that you may regress. Be okay with this and keep moving toward the work. You can never slip too far back. The universe is designed to clean us up and get us back on track.

I pray that you notice when you are emotionally leaning on others a bit too much. Take your legs back.

I pray that you realize that everyone in your life is your teacher.

I pray that you give but not to your detriment. Depleting you and your resources isn't a badge of honor.

I pray that you put yourself first. It's okay to say no, especially if saying yes is harmful to you or takes you off your path.

I pray that you don't let guilt consume you and become your steering influence.

I pray that you stockpile your life's experiences and share your bounty with others in need of encouragement or advice. Your journey can possibly help someone else.

Please pray the same for me.

YOUR PRAYERS

_____

_____

_____

_____

_____

_____

_____

_____

_____

_____

_____

_____

_____

_____

_____

_____

_____

YOUR PRAYERS

YOUR PRAYERS

YOUR PRAYERS

_____

_____

_____

_____

_____

_____

_____

_____

_____

_____

_____

_____

_____

_____

_____

_____

_____

_____

_____

_____

YOUR PRAYERS

_____

_____

_____

_____

_____

_____

_____

_____

_____

_____

_____

_____

_____

_____

_____

_____

_____

YOUR PRAYERS

YOUR PRAYERS

YOUR PRAYERS

YOUR PRAYERS

YOUR PRAYERS

YOUR PRAYERS

_____

_____

_____

_____

_____

_____

_____

_____

_____

_____

_____

_____

_____

_____

_____

_____

_____

_____

YOUR PRAYERS

_____

_____

_____

_____

_____

_____

_____

_____

_____

_____

_____

_____

_____

_____

_____

_____

_____

LEGACY OF LOVE

A legacy of love I bequeath to the joys of my life,
one that started while I carried you inside.

You are two precious jewels that I was chosen to receive.
You are the ones who are rare and special indeed.

We share our trials, joys, and secrets with each other,
the way it should be with daughters and mother.

We've laughed and cried together,
always making our challenges better.

I gained strength in the valley with the help of you two,
many times with prayers and scriptures to bring us through.

You say I'm your hero. I say mine is you.
Without you in my life, it would be hard to endure.

I stand in the limelight and cheer you on,
as I see the accomplishments and how elegantly you have grown.

There was never any doubt that you would achieve your goals. You
question adversity, but you have no fear.
You are like eternal flames that continually glow.

—Janet Matthews Moore

I pray that you show your children in word, thought, and deed how remarkable they are.

I pray that you exercise patience.

I pray that you validate their feelings.

I pray that you nurture their interests.

I pray that you listen to them, hear them, and respect them as human beings.

I pray that you give your child your undivided attention.

I pray that you don't use history to dictate how you should deal with your children. Recognize that your child is not you and what may have been done to you may not work for your child.

I pray that you recognize your children as individuals.

I pray that you continue to take the time to self-reflect for the sake of your children. Working on you helps them.

I pray that you teach your children to be the greatest expression of themselves, no matter what others are doing or saying.

I pray that you teach them to trust their instincts.

I pray that you teach them to dream and to let no one stop them.

I pray you teach them the importance of belief in self.

I pray that you teach them the lessons you didn't learn until later in life. Teach them early.

I pray that your children know that what they say matters and that you encourage their voice and perspective.

I pray that you are honest with your children.

I pray that you teach them early how to set boundaries and how to respect the boundaries of others.

I pray that you nurture your children's confidence.

I pray that you don't force your ideologies and ways of thought on your children; guide them gently.

I pray that you are open enough to realize when your children are teaching you a life lesson.

I pray that you realize that you are an incredible parent. You are doing the best you know how to do with the tools you have.

I pray that you recognize that as you start to peel back the layers and heal those hurting parts of yourself, you in turn begin to heal and emotionally course correct your children. For that reason alone, continue the journey, no matter how rough and bumpy it gets.

Please pray the same for me.

YOUR PRAYERS

YOUR PRAYERS

YOUR PRAYERS

_____

_____

_____

_____

_____

_____

_____

_____

_____

_____

_____

_____

_____

_____

_____

_____

YOUR PRAYERS

_____

_____

_____

_____

_____

_____

_____

_____

_____

_____

_____

_____

_____

_____

_____

_____

_____

_____

YOUR PRAYERS

YOUR PRAYERS

YOUR PRAYERS

YOUR PRAYERS

_____

_____

_____

_____

_____

_____

_____

_____

_____

_____

_____

_____

_____

_____

_____

_____

_____

_____

_____

_____

YOUR PRAYERS

YOUR PRAYERS

_____

_____

_____

_____

_____

_____

_____

_____

_____

_____

_____

_____

_____

_____

_____

_____

_____

YOUR PRAYERS

_____

_____

_____

_____

_____

_____

_____

_____

_____

_____

_____

_____

_____

_____

_____

_____

_____

_____

YOUR PRAYERS

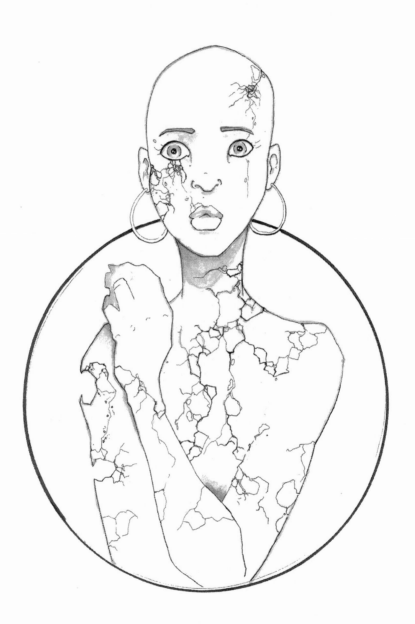

MY SOUL IS
NOT MADE OF STONE

Awakening in the middle of the night with tears streaming down
my face, I returned from my visit to a most wonderful place.

In a brief dream for several minutes or more, I revisited the past
and welcomed that open door, the subconscious refusing to bury
what I thought had been cast out from my life's shore.

Reliving the love you made to me, before my eyes were open to
see, things were back the way they were, just the way I wanted
them to be.

One of the reasons God gave man a soul is so that life's story can
be remembered and, when need be, retold.

As I felt the warmth of your presence and rested in your embrace,
I relived the past; it was no longer erased.

To be able to taste of our time again, when emotions were entwined, gave sweet peace to my mind.

Being grateful for dreams that aid in healing, in a place where I long to roam, by the experience I surely know that my soul is not made of stone.

—Janet Matthews Moore

I pray that you understand just how powerful love is.

I pray that you are committed to love. Let love be the agent that keeps you centered, confident, compassionate, open, and operating at your highest and greatest good.

I pray that you teach others how to love you.

I pray that you give what it is you're lacking in your relationships. Instead of complaining about what you aren't getting, give it.

I pray you always ask yourself, *Am I giving in my role as friend, lover, wife, and mother in the same proportion as what I expect to receive?*

I pray that you understand that the person you love is a reflection of the love you feel for yourself; the love reflecting back to you from that person has its origin in your heart.

I pray that you take in the criticism given to you by someone you love, and instead of getting defensive, breathe it in and say, "Thank you." Lessons are the keys that unlock the many doors into who you are.

I pray that you don't run away from love when someone starts to reveal things about yourself that you don't want to see. Being in relationships with others offers us opportunities to heal those parts of us that need healing.

I pray that you are fine when people don't agree with you. Not everyone will see eye to eye with you on things. Be okay with this.

I pray that you allow love to use you in such a way that it not only heals you but it heals others as well.

I pray that you are selfless in love.

I pray that you don't rush into relationships of any kind. Take your time.

I pray that you take the time to discern what love looks and feels like for you.

I pray that you keep your voice in your relationships while at the same time you are able to release any unyielding, strong-willed ways in order to receive love, grace, and correction.

I pray that independence doesn't blind you. Let your partner play his or her role in the relationship. Doing this takes strength, confidence, and courage.

I pray that you can see yourself in your partner's eyes. This will keep separatism at bay.

I pray that you can see yourself in everyone. This will keep inferiority, inadequacy, jealousy, and a whole host of other things at bay.

I pray that you don't take on responsibility for other people's issues. Let their stuff be their stuff.

I pray that you recognize when others are projecting. Don't let it stick to you. There projections have nothing to do with you.

I pray that when you start to have doubts in your relationships that you address those doubts. Don't sweep them under the rug.

I pray that you watch out for finger-pointing.

I pray that you lovingly deliver whatever communication you need to deliver to whomever you need to deliver it, without being attached to the outcome or his or her response.

I pray you learn to set boundaries.

I pray that you know that forgiving others doesn't mean you let down or release your boundaries.

I pray that you are comfortable telling those you love that you love them and why you love them.

I pray that you don't hold back from showing affection because you fear rejection.

I pray that you stay open to love—that even when you feel like shutting down, you brace yourself for impact and remain open. Love freely and deeply, not worrying if you will receive love back.

I pray that you have compassion for others, no matter how they act toward you. If their actions bother you, use that as a meter, a ruler, or a guide to help you clean up things within yourself.

I pray that you listen when others speak. Be interested in their point of view, not just your own.

I pray that you don't allow the actions of others to dictate your actions. Remain true and solid.

I pray that when you feel yourself acting or making decisions based on someone else, you notice and reevaluate.

I pray that you release the need to be the center of attention.

I pray that you don't feel depleted when others don't give you back the same amount of attention. Feed off of your own light. Validate and own who you are for yourself. Be your own stamp of approval.

I pray that you give others their due. It doesn't take anything away from you to praise someone else.

I pray that you allow yourself to be genuinely interested in others.

I pray that you don't always think others are out to get you and you become so untrusting that you can't see friendship surrounding you.

I pray that you recognize when you are in character, playing the victim.

I pray that you give *yourself* the same amount of love that you give to others, if not more.

I pray that you let love order your steps. Love will take you to the exact place in your life you need to be. Inject it into every capacity of your being.

I pray that you ask yourself regularly,

"Am I operating in *fear of love*?"

I pray that you shift from wanting people to change to wanting people to be the best they can be for themselves.

In all these things, please pray the same for me.

ACKNOWLEDGMENTS

There are many people who have inspired me on this journey of writing my first book through example, word, or quiet observation. I've been nudged and pushed through this entire process. I have endured, have welcomed, and am thankful for the bruises. To my teachers, Mary Herndon and Dr. Guldal Caba—Mary, I see you at the shore waving; Guldal, thank you for making me feel safe, nurtured, and loved. Thank you for unraveling me. To my aunts Linda Caldwell and Jackie Mobley, you guys are carrying the torch. I love you for your honesty and candor to discovering the meaning behind the journey. To Monica, my sister, thanks for being there and for being so honest and real with me, no matter what. It's healing time! Granddaddy Britt, you rock! I have so much respect and adoration for you and your journey. You are so brave and such a strong, honest, giving man. I'm proud and honored to call you Granddaddy Britt. Uncle Namon, we have always had a special bond; no matter how far apart we are when I need you, you are there. I love you. To the Blackbirds, my Roc's, my backbone when I need one, my voices of reason, my support system and my guides. You guys are my sisters for life. I love you the mostest. Roda, thank you, thank you, thank you for your encouragement, your confidence in me, and your ability to see behind my veil. You are an incredible writer, a superb editor, and the best "pusher" anyone could have in their corner. To my strong, smart, driven, beautiful husband, I love all that you are, every aspect of you—*everything*. Thank you for being my mirror. Thank you for pushing me and showing me what it looks like to be confident, secure, and loved. Thank you for your honor, integrity, and loyalty. Thank you, Arlene, for giving him breathing room to become the man he is today. River, you are my lighter side reflected. God couldn't have created a better human being to be my son. I am truly honored to call myself River's mom. I love you more than the entire universe. I love you more than infinity and beyond. I'll go off of the edge of the earth for you—top that!

Thank you, Mom, for leaving your soul print in so many different ways, from your book of poetry to your recipes for life and food. I hope that I'm magnifying your name and you are sitting in heaven, saying, "Yay, Keta!"

Written to: Andrae Crouch: *The Best Of*, Eva Cassidy: *Songbird*, Nina Simone: *The Very Best of 1967-1972*, Keith Jarrett: *The Koln Concert (Live)*, Isaak Hayes, The O'Jays, Gladys Knight: *Soundtrack to Claudine*, and a little Bob Marley here and there.

YOUR PRAYERS

_____

_____

_____

_____

_____

_____

_____

_____

_____

_____

_____

_____

_____

_____

_____

YOUR PRAYERS

YOUR PRAYERS

YOUR PRAYERS

YOUR PRAYERS

YOUR PRAYERS

_____

_____

_____

_____

_____

_____

_____

_____

_____

_____

_____

_____

_____

_____

_____

_____

_____

YOUR PRAYERS

_____

_____

_____

_____

_____

_____

_____

_____

_____

_____

_____

_____

_____

_____

_____

_____

_____

_____

_____

_____

YOUR PRAYERS

_____

_____

_____

_____

_____

_____

_____

_____

_____

_____

_____

_____

_____

_____

_____

_____

_____

YOUR PRAYERS

_____

_____

_____

_____

_____

_____

_____

_____

_____

_____

_____

_____

_____

_____

_____

_____

_____

YOUR PRAYERS

YOUR PRAYERS